D1391959

Contents

Entertaining

Anne Ager

Green devil

Sufficient for 1 cocktail
Preparation time: 4 minutes

1 ½ tablespoons Crème de
    Menthe

3 tablespoons vodka

juice of ½ lime

2 tablespoons crushed ice

To garnish:

twist of lime peel

small sprig of fresh mint

Few people possess a cocktail shaker, and you can mix a very successful cocktail without one. All you need is a screw-top jar, such as a clean empty coffee jar, and a tea strainer!

1. Put the Crème de Menthe, vodka and lime juice into a cocktail shaker or clean screw-top jar with the crushed ice.
2. Shake thoroughly for at least 30 seconds, then strain into a stemmed cocktail glass.
3. Garnish with lime peel and mint and serve immediately.

Sunset special

Sufficient for 1 cocktail
Preparation time: 3 minutes

1 tablespoon red vermouth

1 tablespoon Orange Curaçao or
    Cointreau

2 tablespoons gin

2 tablespoons crushed ice

thin slice of orange, to garnish

1. Put the red vermouth, Orange Curaçao and gin into a cocktail shaker or clean screw-top jar with the crushed ice.
2. Shake thoroughly for at least 30 seconds, and strain into a stemmed cocktail glass.
3. Garnish with a slice of orange and serve immediately.

Highland hopper

Sufficient for 1 cocktail
Preparation time: 3 minutes

2 tablespoons whisky

2 tablespoons dry Dubonnet
(or any extra dry white
vermouth)

1 teaspoon lemon juice

2 tablespoons crushed ice

twist of lemon peel, to garnish

1. Put the whisky, dry Dubonnet and lemon juice into a cocktail shaker or clean screw-top jar with the crushed ice.
2. Shake thoroughly for at least 30 seconds, and strain into a stemmed cocktail glass.
3. Garnish with a twist of lemon peel and serve immediately.

Tall story

Sufficient for 1 cocktail
Preparation time; 3 minutes

3 tablespoons brandy

1 tablespoon ginger wine

2-3 ice cubes

150 ml/¼ pint sparkling
mineral water

To garnish:

1 green grape

3 cloves

1. Put the brandy, ginger wine and ice cubes into a tall, slim, straight-sided glass (highball glass).
2. Top up with well chilled sparkling mineral water.
3. Stud the grape with the cloves, add to the cocktail and serve immediately.

Curried salmon balls

Makes 24
Preparation time: 25-30 minutes, plus chilling time
Cooking time: 2-3 minutes

1 x 200 g/7 oz can pink salmon, drained

75 g/3 oz fresh white breadcrumbs

3 teaspoons curry powder

2 eggs

grated rind of ½ lemon

salt

freshly ground black pepper

6 tablespoons dried white breadcrumbs

oil for deep frying

These may be eaten either hot or cold, with a piquant mayonnaise dip, made of mayonnaise mixed with tomato purée to taste, salt and pepper, and a little finely chopped gherkin.

1. Mix the canned salmon with the fresh breadcrumbs, 1 teaspoon of the curry powder, and the eggs, lemon rind, and salt and pepper to taste. Chill for 1 hour.
2. Form the mixture into 24 small balls, about the size of a large grape.
3. Roll the salmon balls in the dried breadcrumbs, to give an even coating.
4. Lower the salmon balls into a pan of hot deep oil and fry for about 2-3 minutes, until crisp and golden.
5. Drain the salmon balls thoroughly, then sprinkle with the remaining curry powder.
6. Spike the salmon balls with wooden cocktail sticks.

Anchovy fingers

Makes 48
Preparation time: 20-25 minutes
Cooking time: 6 minutes
Oven: 220°C, 425°F, Gas Mark 7

1 x 370 g/13 oz packet frozen puff pastry, thawed

1 x 25 g/1 oz jar anchovy paste

1 small onion, peeled and grated

freshly ground black pepper

1 egg, beaten

3 tablespoons grated Parmesan cheese

cayenne pepper

1. Roll out the pastry thinly to a rectangle 40 cm x 30 cm/16 inches x 12 inches. Cut into two equal sized rectangles, 20 cm x 30 cm/8 inches x 12 inches.
2. Spread one pastry rectangle with the anchovy paste. Sprinkle with the grated onion and season with black pepper.
3. Brush one side of the remaining pastry rectangle with beaten egg, and place egg side down over the anchovy paste. Roll the two pastry layers lightly together.
4. Cut in half to give two rectangles about 10 cm x 30 cm/4 inches x 12 inches. Brush with beaten egg and sprinkle with the grated Parmesan cheese.
5. Cut through at 1 cm/½ inch intervals to give fingers 10 cm x 1 cm/4 inches x ½ inch. Either leave the fingers flat, or twist them as for cheese straws.
6. Place on lightly greased baking sheets and bake in a preheated oven for about 6 minutes, until golden. Serve hot, sprinkled with cayenne.

Smoked mussel and egg canapés

Makes 24
Preparation time: 12-15 minutes, plus cooling time
Cooking time: 2-3 minutes

4 eggs
salt
freshly ground black pepper
90 g/3½ oz butter
4 tablespoons mayonnaise
2 tablespoons chopped chives
24 small pumpernickel rounds
To garnish:
2 x 75 g/3 oz cans smoked mussels, drained
fronds of dill

The scrambled egg mixture can be prepared well in advance, but the actual canapés are best assembled just before needed.

1. Beat the eggs with salt and pepper. Heat 40 g/1½ oz of the butter in a pan and add the beaten egg. Cook stirring, over a gentle heat, until the mixture forms soft, creamy flakes.
2. Allow the scrambled egg mixture to cool slightly. Stir in the mayonnaise and chives and leave to become quite cold.
3. Spread the pumpernickel rounds lightly with the remaining butter, and top each round with a little of the egg mixture.
4. Garnish each canapé with a smoked mussel and a small sprig of dill.

Roquefort canapés

Makes 30
Preparation time: 20 minutes

5 slices wholemeal bread, from a large sliced loaf
100 g/4 oz butter, softened
175 g/6 oz Roquefort or other blue cheese, crumbled
3 tablespoons brandy
75 g/3 oz walnuts, finely chopped .
salt
freshly ground black pepper
30 small black or green grapes, to garnish

1. Remove the crusts from the bread and cut each slice into 6 even rectangles, making 30 small rectangles.
2. Mix the softened butter with the crumbled Roquefort cheese, brandy, nuts and salt and pepper to taste.
3. Mound the mixture decoratively on each square of bread.
4. Garnish each canapé with a grape, peeled or unpeeled according to preference.

Variation:
Walnut halves can be sandwiched with the Roquefort mixture, and then one placed on each rectangle of lightly buttered bread. Sprinkle with a little paprika or chopped fresh parsley.

Sherried onion soup

Serves 6
Preparation time: 8 minutes
Cooking time: 25 minutes

3 large onions, peeled and thinly sliced

75 g/3 oz butter

30 g/1 oz plain flour

1 litre/1¾ pints beef stock

2 teaspoons brown sugar

salt

freshly ground black pepper

150 ml/¼ pint medium sweet sherry

3 slices bread, from a large sliced loaf

3 tablespoons grated Parmesan cheese

1. Fry the onions very gently in 50 g/2 oz of the butter until they soften and turn golden.
2. Stir in the flour and cook for 1 minute. Gradually stir in the beef stock and bring to the boil. Simmer for 3 minutes.
3. Add the sugar, salt, pepper and sherry, and simmer for a further 10 minutes. (The soup can be made to this stage in advance, and then reheated when needed.)
4. Remove the crusts from the bread. Spread with the remaining butter and sprinkle with the grated Parmesan cheese.
5. Grill until the bread slices are golden. Cut into small squares or triangles. These can be made in advance and warmed through in a moderate oven.
6. Serve the soup accompanied by the hot cheese toasts.

Watercress and orange soup

Serves 6
Preparation time: 15 minutes, plus chilling time
Cooking time: 20 minutes

3 bunches watercress

1 large onion, peeled and finely chopped

50 g/2 oz butter

40 g/1½ oz plain flour

600 ml/1 pint chicken stock

300 ml/½ pint milk

grated rind of 2 oranges

3 tablespoons orange juice

salt

freshly ground black pepper

150 ml/¼ pint soured cream

To garnish:

1 orange, cut into thin slices

small sprigs of watercress

1. Trim and discard the stalk ends from the watercress. Wash the watercress and shake dry.
2. Fry the onion gently in the butter for 3 minutes. Add the watercress and cook together for a further 3 minutes.
3. Stir in the flour and cook for 1 minute. Gradually stir in the chicken stock. Bring to the boil and add the milk, orange rind and juice, and salt and pepper to taste.
4. Simmer gently for 10 minutes.
5. Allow the soup to cool and then blend in the liquidizer with the soured cream until smooth.
6. Alternatively rub the vegetable mixture through a sieve, then stir in the soured cream.
7. Chill the soup for at least 4 hours before serving.
8. Garnish each portion of soup with a slice of orange and a sprig of watercress.

Salmon and cheese pâté

Serves 6
Preparation time: 35 minutes, plus chilling

1 x 200 g/7 oz can pink salmon

175 g/6 oz full fat soft cheese

salt

freshly ground black pepper

1 garlic clove, peeled and crushed

juice of ½ lemon

50 g/2 oz melted butter

1 teaspoon powdered gelatine

1 tablespoon hot water

To garnish:

150 ml/¼ pint single cream

2 tablespoons lumpfish roe

1 lemon, cut into thin wedges

sprigs of parsley

1. Put the canned salmon (undrained) into a bowl with the cheese, salt, pepper, garlic and lemon juice. Pound together until quite smooth. Stir in the melted butter.
2. Dissolve the gelatine in the water and stir into the salmon mixture.
3. Once the mixture starts to stiffen, spoon into 6 oiled heart-shaped moulds (such as those used for coeurs à la crème) or into small individual soufflé dishes. Chill for 2-3 hours until set.
4. Unmould each individual pâté on to a small plate. Spoon over a little cream and garnish with lumpfish roe, lemon and parsley. Serve with toast or hot bread.

Chicken liver and tomato croustades

Serves 6
Preparation time: 20 minutes
Cooking time: about 25 minutes

6 large slices bread, each 2.5 cm/1 inch thick

oil for deep frying

50 g/2 oz butter

1 medium onion, peeled and finely chopped

225 g/8 oz chicken livers, chopped

1 tablespoon plain flour

150 ml/¼ pint dry sherry

8 tomatoes, peeled, seeded and chopped

1 garlic clove, peeled and crushed

salt

freshly ground black pepper

chopped fresh parsley, to garnish

The bread cases can be prepared and fried in advance, and then reheated in a moderate oven when needed.

1. Using a 9 cm/3½ inch pastry cutter, or a small saucer as a guide, cut a circle from each slice of bread.
2. Carefully hollow out some of the centre crumb from each bread circle, so that it looks like a vol-au-vent case.
3. Deep fry the bread cases in hot oil until they are crisp and golden, about 3 minutes. Drain on absorbent paper and keep warm.
4. Melt the butter in a saucepan. Add the chopped onion and cook for 3 minutes. Add the chicken livers and cook in the butter until they start to colour.
5. Stir in the flour and cook for 1 minute. Add the sherry, chopped tomato, garlic and salt and pepper to taste. Cover and simmer for 10 minutes.
6. Spoon the chicken liver mixture into the hot bread cases and sprinkle each one with chopped parsley. Serve immediately.

Blue cheese mille feuilles

Serves 12-14
Preparation time: 35-40 minutes, plus cooling time
Cooking time: 15-20 minutes
Oven: 220°C, 425°F, Gas Mark 7

2 x 370 g/13 oz packets frozen puff pastry, thawed

beaten egg

4 tablespoons grated Parmesan cheese

375 g/12 oz Ricotta cheese or sieved cottage cheese

225 g/8 oz Danish blue cheese, crumbled

4 tablespoons thick mayonnaise

100 g/4 oz walnuts, finely chopped

1 medium onion, peeled and grated

salt

freshly ground black pepper

These savoury mille feuilles are best if assembled no more than 2 hours in advance.

1. Roll out the pastry quite thinly into two rectangles, each 25 cm x 20 cm/10 inches x 8 inches. Cut each one in half lengthways, to give four rectangles each 25 cm x 10 cm/ 10 inches x 4 inches.
2. Place the rectangles of puff pastry on to two baking sheets which have been lightly brushed with oil. Brush the top of the pastry with beaten egg, and sprinkle with the Parmesan cheese.
3. Bake the pastry layers in a preheated oven for 15-20 minutes, until golden.
4. Remove the baked pastry layers to a wire rack and leave to cool.
5. Mix the ricotta cheese with the blue cheese, mayonnaise, walnuts and onion, and add salt and pepper to taste.
6. Turn two of the pastry layers so that the flat surfaces are uppermost. Spread each one with half of the cheese filling. Sandwich together with the other two pastry layers.

Seafood tomatoes

Serves 13
Preparation time: 35 minutes

12 large firm tomatoes

225 g/8 oz cooked white crabmeat (frozen or canned)

175 g/6 oz shelled, cooked mussels

150 ml/¼ pint soured cream

2 tablespoons dry vermouth

salt

freshly ground black pepper

1 x 58 g/2 oz jar lumpfish roe

watercress or shredded lettuce, to serve

1. Cut a thin slice from the stalk end of each tomato. Carefully hollow out the centre of each tomato with a grapefruit spoon.
2. Turn the hollowed tomatoes upside down on absorbent paper to drain.
3. Flake the crabmeat. If the mussels are very large, cut them in half.
4. Mix the soured cream with the vermouth and salt and pepper to taste. Stir in the crabmeat and mussels.
5. Fill each hollowed tomato with the fish mixture and top with a little lumpfish roe.
6. Arrange the filled tomatoes on a bed of watercress or shredded lettuce.

Ham tartare-style

Serves 12
Preparation time: 45-50 minutes

900 g/2 lb cooked ham, off the bone

1 medium onion, peeled and finely chopped or grated

150 ml/¼ pint olive oil

juice of 1 lemon

1 tablespoon caster sugar

1 tablespoon French mustard

8 anchovy fillets, finely chopped

1 tablespoon Worcestershire sauce

2 garlic cloves, peeled and crushed

4 tablespoons chopped fresh parsley

salt

freshly ground black pepper

To garnish:

2 hard boiled eggs

sprigs of parsley

To serve:

4 tablespoons capers

1 medium onion, peeled and finely chopped

4 tomatoes, cut into sections

75 g/3 oz black olives

1. Mince the ham finely and put into a bowl with the chopped onion.

2. Mix the olive oil with the lemon juice, sugar, mustard, anchovy fillets, Worcestershire sauce, garlic, chopped parsley, and salt and pepper to taste.

3. Stir the flavoured oil dressing into the ham, so that the meat is well moistened. If you are making this dish well in advance, then be a little more generous with the quantity of dressing.

4. Separate the hard boiled egg yolks from the whites. Sieve the egg yolks and finely chop the whites.

5. Spoon the minced ham mixture into the centre of a large serving platter, leaving a border around the edge for the serving accompaniments.

6. Sprinkle the sieved egg yolk and chopped egg white over the ham mixture. Arrange small mounds of capers, chopped onion, tomato and olives around the edge of the dish.

7. Serve either with crusty bread, or with fingers of toast spread with parsley butter.

Lettuce and prawn parcels

Serves 12
Preparation time: 35 minutes, plus chilling time

8 hard boiled eggs

225 g/8 oz full fat soft cheese

6 spring onions, finely chopped

4 tablespoons thick mayonnaise

450 g/1 lb peeled prawns, chopped

salt

freshly ground black pepper

24 large lettuce leaves

Dressing:

300 ml/½ pint olive oil

grated rind and juice of 1 lemon

1 tablespoon white wine vinegar

1 teaspoon caster sugar

1 garlic clove, crushed

3 tablespoons chopped fresh parsley

6 gherkins, finely chopped (optional)

3 tablespoons chopped fresh chives

1. Shell the hard boiled eggs and chop them roughly.
2. Mix the chopped egg with the cheese, chopped spring onion, mayonnaise, prawns, and salt and pepper to taste. Chill well for 1 hour.
3. Mould the prawn and egg mixture into 12 even portions, and completely enclose each one in two lettuce leaves, like a parcel.
4. Arrange the lettuce and prawn parcels neatly in a serving dish, making sure that any loose edges of lettuce are tucked well underneath.
5. For the dressing, mix all the ingredients together and spoon over the parcels. Cover with cling wrap and chill for 3-4 hours before serving. The dish can be prepared the night before without any risk of spoiling.
6. Garnish the dish with a few unpeeled prawns.

Turkey mayonnaise

Serves 12
Preparation time: 50 minutes, plus chilling time
Cooking time: 35 minutes

12 small turkey fillets

seasoned flour

beaten egg

fine dried breadcrumbs

175 g/6 oz butter

4 tablespoons oil

Sauce:

300 ml/½ pint mayonnaise

300 ml/½ pint soured cream

3 tablespoons grated onion

coarsely grated rind of 2 oranges

2 tablespoons chopped fresh mint

1. Place the turkey fillets between two sheets of lightly oiled foil and batten out with a meat mallet or rolling pin until thin.
2. Dust each turkey escalope lightly with seasoned flour. Dip into beaten egg and then coat with breadcrumbs.
3. Heat half the butter and the oil in a large shallow pan. Add three of the prepared escalopes and cook for 4 minutes on each side. Drain.
4. Cook the remaining escalopes, adding more butter and oil to the pan.
5. When cool, wrap the escalopes in cling film and chill until needed.
6. For the sauce, mix all the ingredients together, adding a little hot water to give a smooth coating consistency.
7. Arrange the turkey escalopes on a serving dish and spoon over the sauce.

Plaice Madras

Serves 12
Serves 12
**Preparation time: 45 minutes, plus
chilling time**
Cooking time: 15 minutes

12 small plaice fillets

4 bananas

juice of 1 lemon

1 medium onion, peeled and
   finely chopped

50 g/2 oz butter

300 ml/½ pint dry cider

salt

freshly ground black pepper

300 ml/½ pint mayonnaise

300 ml/½ pint soured cream

1 tablespoon hot Madras curry
   powder

50 g/2 oz sultanas

To garnish:

1 red pepper, finely chopped

thin slices of lemon

1. Skin the fillets if the fishmonger has not already done so.

2. Peel the bananas and cut each one into 3 even size pieces. Brush all over with lemon juice.

3. Put a piece of banana on to each plaice fillet and roll up, securing with a wooden cocktail stick.

4. Fry the onion gently in the butter in a large shallow pan for 2-3 minutes. Arrange the rolled fish fillets on top. Pour over the cider and season to taste. Cover the pan with a lid and poach gently for 10-12 minutes, until the fish is tender.

5. Remove the fish fillets with a slotted spoon and place on a serving dish. Strain the cooking liquid and reserve for the sauce.

6. Mix the mayonnaise with the soured cream, curry powder and sultanas.
Add sufficient of the fish stock to give a smooth coating consistency. Taste and adjust the seasoning.

7. Spoon the curry mayonnaise evenly over the cooked fish fillets and chill thoroughly.

8. Garnish with the finely chopped red pepper and lemon slices.

Drunken chocolate cake

Serves 12
Preparation time: 1 hour 40 minutes,
plus chilling time
Cooking time: 20 minutes
Oven: 200°C, 400°F, Gas Mark 6

8 eggs

275 g/10 oz caster sugar

finely grated rind of 1 orange

175 g/6 oz self-raising flour

50 g/2 oz cocoa powder

6 tablespoons Grand Marnier

Filling:

175 g/6 oz plain chocolate

450 ml/³/₄ pint double or
 whipping cream

2 tablespoons Grand Marnier

To glaze:

225 g/8 oz orange jelly
 marmalade

6 tablespoons water

2 thin skinned oranges, thinly
 sliced

174 g/6 oz plain chocolate,
 coarsely grated, to decorate

1. Line 2 large Swiss roll tins, 25 cm x 35 cm/10 inch x 14 inch with greased greaseproof paper.

2. Put the eggs, sugar and orange rind into a large bowl. Stand over a saucepan of hot water and whisk until the mixture is thick, pale and foamy. Alternatively this can be done in an electric mixer.

3. Fold in the sifted flour and cocoa powder. Pour into the prepared tins, spreading the mixture evenly.

4. Bake in a preheated oven for about 10 minutes until firm but spongy to the touch.

5. Turn the sponge layers out on to wire racks. Sprinkle with the Grand Marnier and leave to cool.

6. Divide each sponge layer into two lengthways, so that you have four layers each measuring 13 cm x 35 cm/5 inches x 14 inches.

7. To make the filling, break the chocolate into pieces and melt in a bowl over a pan of hot water. Allow to cool slightly. Whip the cream until it is thick and stir in the melted chocolate and Grand Marnier.

8. Sandwich the four sponge layers together with the chocolate cream filling.

9. To make the glaze, sieve the marmalade into a saucepan and add the water. Bring to the boil, stirring. Add the orange slices and simmer for 10 minutes.

10. Lift the orange slices out of the glaze and place on a piece of greased greaseproof paper.

11. Allow the glaze to cool a little, then spread or brush evenly over the top and sides of the cake. Arrange the orange slices on top, and glaze the top of the cake once more.

12. Coat the sides of the cake with coarsely grated chocolate. Chill.

Coffee and chestnut parfait

Serves 12
Preparation time: 20 minutes, plus chilling time

3 x 425 g/15 oz cans
  unsweetened chestnut purée

2 tablespoons powdered instant
  coffee

150 ml/¼ pint boiling water

175 g/6 oz caster sugar

450 ml/¾ pint double or
  whipping cream

To decorate:

300 ml/½ pint double or
  whipping cream

12 marrons glacé

12 tablespoons Tia Maria,
  optional

sponge fingers or crêpes
  d'entelles, to serve

1. Put the chestnut purée into a bowl and mash with a wooden spoon.
2. Dissolve the instant coffee in the boiling water and beat into the chestnut purée, together with the caster sugar.
3. Whip the cream until it is quite thick and fold lightly but thoroughly into the chestnut mixture.
4. Spoon the parfait into 12 tall stemmed glasses and chill.
5. Pipe a swirl of whipped cream on each parfait and top with a marrons glacé. For a really special occasion, pour a tablespoon of Tia Maria over each one. Serve with small sponge fingers or crêpes d'entelles.

Raspberry jellied shortcake

Serves 12
Preparation time: 1 hour, plus chilling time
Cooking time: 40 minutes
Oven: 180°C, 350°F, Gas Mark 4

225 g/8 oz unsalted butter

100 g/4 oz caster sugar

grated rind of 1 orange

225 g/8 oz self-raising flour

100 g/4 oz cornflour

3 packets raspberry-flavoured jelly

6 tablespoons brandy

10 large strawberries, hulled and halved

450 g/1 lb raspberries and chopped strawberries, mixed

To decorate:

450 ml/³⁄₄ pint double or whipping cream, whipped

few whole strawberries, hulled

1. Soften the butter in a mixing bowl. Beat in the sugar and orange rind until the mixture is light and fluffy.
2. Sift the flour and cornflour and work into the butter and sugar mixture. Knead to a smooth dough. Chill for 30 minutes.
3. Lightly grease a 30 cm/12 inch round loose-bottomed cake tin. Press the shortcake dough in an even layer over the base of the tin.
4. Bake the shortcake in a preheated oven for 40 minutes. Remove from the oven and leave the shortcake to cool in the tin. If the shortcake happens to have risen unevenly, level it off with a sharp knife.
5. Divide the packet jellies into sections and put into a bowl with 600 ml/1 pint boiling water. Stir to dissolve the jelly.
6. Make up the liquid jelly to 1.25 litres/ 2¼ pints with cold water. Stir in the brandy. Chill the jelly until it becomes syrupy.
7. Dip the halved strawberries one at a time into the syrupy jelly and arrange around the inner sides of the cake tin. Put into the freezer for a few minutes to 'set' the strawberries in position. Alternatively, place in the refrigerator for about 20 minutes.
8. Stir half the mixed raspberries and all the strawberries into the remaining syrupy jelly and pour carefully into the cake tin.
9. Chill the jellied shortcake until the jelly layer is quite firm.
10. Carefully ease the sides of the set jelly away from the tin, and lift the complete shortcake out on its tin base.
11. Swirl the whipped cream on top of the jellied shortcake, or pipe decoratively. Decorate with the remaining raspberries and the whole strawberries.

Chinese leaves and grape salad

Serves 10-12
Preparation time: 30 minutes, plus chilling time

350 g/12 oz full fat soft cheese

100 g/4 oz nibbed almonds, toasted

1 medium head Chinese leaves

350 g/12 oz green grapes, skinned (and pipped if preferred)

4 sticks celery, finely chopped

6 rings canned pineapple, chopped

Dressing:

150 ml/³⁄₄ pint soured cream

2 tablespoons canned pineapple syrup

juice of ½ lemon

salt

freshly ground black pepper

3 tablespoons chopped fresh parsley or chives

1. Form the cheese into small balls about the size of an olive. Roll in toasted nuts to give an even coating, and chill for 1 hour.
2. Separate the leaves from the head of Chinese leaves. Wash and shake dry.
3. Tear the Chinese leaves into pieces and put into a large salad bowl. Add the grapes, celery and pineapple.
4. For the dressing, mix the soured cream with the pineapple syrup, lemon juice, salt and pepper to taste, and the chopped parsley.
5. Add to the prepared salad ingredients and toss lightly together.
6. Scatter the cream cheese balls in amongst the salad.
7. Alternatively, arrange the salad in a more formal manner, on a flat platter, separating each ingredient.

Endive and anchovy salad

Serves 12
Preparation time: 30 minutes

2 heads of endive

6 medium courgettes

225 g/8 oz button mushrooms, thinly sliced

75 g/3 oz stuffed olives, sliced

Dressing:

150 ml/¼ pint olive oil

3 x 50 g/2 oz cans anchovy fillets

juice of 1 lemon

freshly ground black pepper

1 garlic clove, peeled and crushed

grated Parmesan cheese, to serve

1. Wash the heads of endive and shake dry. Separate the leaves from the main stalk and put into a large salad bowl.
2. Remove both ends from each courgette. Using a mandolin, if you have one, or a very sharp knife, cut the courgettes into very thin slices.
3. Add the sliced courgettes, mushrooms and olives to the endive.
4. For the dressing mix the olive oil with 2 of the cans of anchovy fillets finely chopped, the lemon juice, pepper and garlic.
5. Stir into the prepared salad vegetables and toss together.
6. Arrange the remaining anchovy fillets on top of the salad and serve with a bowl of Parmesan cheese for sprinkling over the top.

Trout en croûte

Serves 6
Preparation time: 1 hour, plus chilling time
Cooking time: 35-40 minutes
Oven: 220°C, 425°F, Gas Mark 7;
190°C, 375°F, Gas Mark 5

100 g/4 oz softened butter

grated rind of 1 lemon

2 tablespoons chopped fresh chives

salt

freshly ground black pepper

2 x 370 g/13 oz packets frozen puff pastry, thawed

3 plump trout, filleted (see below)

beaten egg

Sauce:

3 tablespoons lemon juice

1 teaspoon crushed peppercorns

175 g/6 oz butter

2 tablespoons capers

salt

freshly ground black pepper

1. Mix the softened butter with the lemon rind, chives, and salt and pepper to taste.
2. Put the flavoured butter on to a piece of greaseproof paper and roll up into a 'sausage'. Chill or freeze until firm.
3. Cut a simple fish shape from a piece of thin card. The cut-out fish shape must be large enough to take a whole trout fillet, still leaving a 1 cm/½ inch border the whole way round.
4. Roll out the puff pastry thinly, and, using your cut-out fish shape as a guide, cut out 12 'pastry fish'. Arrange 6 of them, well-spaced out, on a large lightly greased baking sheet.
5. Lay a trout fillet down the centre of each pastry fish, and brush the pastry rim with beaten egg.
6. Cut the chilled flavoured butter into thin slices and arrange one or two on each fish fillet. Lay the remaining pastry fish over the fish fillets, so that they match up in shape to those underneath.
7. Pinch the pastry edges together to seal, making sure that you do not spoil the overall shape of the 'fish'.
8. Glaze with the beaten egg and decorate with a few pastry fins cut from the pastry trimmings. Glaze once more with beaten egg. Make a small hole in the top of each fish to allow the air to escape.
9. Bake in a preheated oven at the higher temperature for 10 minutes, then reduce the temperature and cook for a further 25-30 minutes.
10. To make the sauce, put the lemon juice and peppercorns into a pan. Boil briskly until reduced by half. Add the butter and continue heating until a nutty brown. Stir in the capers and salt and pepper to taste.
11. Arrange the trout en croûte on a serving platter and take to the table with the hot brown butter sauce in a jug – widen the hole in the top of each pastry fish and pour in a little of the sauce as you serve it.

Pork in two mustards and tarragon sauce

Serves 6
Preparation time: 20 minutes
Cooking time: 40 minutes

1 kg/2¼ lb pork fillet

1 large onion, peeled and sliced

100 g/4 oz butter

2 tablespoons oil

1 tablespoon plain flour

300 ml/½ pint Guinness

1 tablespoon English mustard

1 tablespoon mild French
  mustard

1 tablespoon chopped fresh
  tarragon

1 teaspoon caster sugar

salt

freshly ground black pepper

150 ml/¼ pint double cream

3 slices white bread

few sprigs of fresh tarragon, to
  garnish

1. Remove all trace of fat from the pork fillets and trim them into a neat shape. Cut into round slices, about 5 mm/¼ inch thick.
2. Fry the onion in half the butter and the oil in a large shallow pan for 3-4 minutes.
3. Add the pork slices to the pan and continue frying until the meat is coloured on all sides.
4. Stir in the flour and then gradually add the Guinness. Bring to the boil, stirring, and add the mustards, tarragon, sugar, and salt and pepper to taste.
5. Cover and simmer gently for 30 minutes, until the meat is tender.
6. Meanwhile, remove the crusts from the bread, and cut each slice into 8 triangles. Fry the bread triangles in the remaining butter until crisp and golden.
7. Stir the cream into the pork and heat through. Spoon on to a serving dish and arrange the bread croûtons around the edge. Garnish with a few sprigs of fresh tarragon.

Chicken ratatouille

Serves 6
Preparation time: 30 minutes
Cooking time: 1½ hours
Oven: 190°C, 375°F, Gas Mark 5

2 medium aubergines

1 large onion, peeled and thinly
  sliced

1 large red pepper, seeds
  removed, cut into strips

1 large green pepper, seeds
  removed, cut into strips

6 tablespoons oil

2 garlic cloves, crushed

1 x 400 g/14 oz can peeled
  tomatoes

2 teaspoons cornflour

6 chicken breasts, boned and
  skinned

50 g/2 oz butter

100 g/4 oz grated cheese

1. Cut the aubergines into quarters lengthways, and chop into even sized pieces.
2. Fry the onion gently in the oil for 2-3 minutes. Stir in the tomatoes and add salt and pepper to taste. Cover the pan and simmer gently for 40 minutes.
3. Blend the cornflour with a little water and stir into the ratatouille to thicken it lightly. (The ratatouille can be prepared well in advance.)
4. Flatten the chicken breasts slightly with a meat mallet or rolling pin.
5. Heat the butter in a large shallow pan. Add the chicken breasts and fry gently until golden on all sides.
6. Put the ratatouille into a shallow ovenproof serving dish. Arrange the fried chicken breasts on top and sprinkle with the grated cheese. Cook in a preheated oven for 30 minutes.

Beef tournedos with asparagus sauce

Serves 6
Preparation time: 30 minutes, plus chilling time
Cooking time: 25 minutes

6 fillet steaks, each 2.5 cm/1 inch thick

150 ml/¼ pint dry white wine

1 tablespoon chopped fresh basil

1 garlic clove, peeled and crushed

salt

freshly ground black pepper

6 slices white bread

150 g/5 oz butter

2 tablespoons oil

1 x 350 g/12 oz can asparagus spears, drained

150 ml/¼ pint soured cream

fresh basil or watercress, to garnish

1. Put the steaks into a shallow dish and add the wine, basil, garlic, salt and pepper to taste. Cover with cling film and chill for at least 8 hours or overnight.
2. Stamp out an oval from each slice of bread, slightly larger in area than the steaks.
3. Heat 75 g/3 oz of the butter in a shallow pan and add the cut out bread shapes. Fry gently until lightly crisp and golden on both sides. Remove the bread croûtons from the pan and drain on absorbent paper. Keep warm.
4. Add the remaining butter and the oil to the pan, and place over a moderate heat.
5. Drain the steaks from their marinade and add to the hot fat in the pan. Fry for approximately 5 minutes on each side; this will give a medium done steak.
6. Meanwhile put the drained asparagus spears, soured cream and the steak marinade into a liquidizer and blend for 30 seconds. Heat through in a saucepan.
7. Once the steaks are cooked to the desired degree, arrange the fried bread on a serving platter. Put a cooked steak on top of each one and spoon over a little of the asparagus sauce. Garnish with basil or watercress and serve any remaining sauce separately.

Lamb amandine

Serves 6
Preparation time: 25 minutes, plus
chilling time
Cooking time: 1 hour
Oven: 190°C, 375°F, Gas Mark 5

2 best end of neck lamb joints
  (6 bones on each joint)

juice of 2 lemons

4 tablespoons olive oil

1 garlic clove, peeled and
  crushed

2 tablespoons chopped fresh
  parsley

salt

freshly ground black pepper

20 split almonds

Sauce:

3 egg yolks

300 ml/½ pint olive oil

grated rind of 2 lemons

50 g/2 oz ground almonds

2 garlic cloves, peeled and
  crushed

pinch of caster sugar

salt

freshly ground black pepper

sprigs of watercress, to garnish

1. Ask your butcher to prepare the lamb joints for you; removing the skin and scraping the bones clean.
2. Put the prepared lamb joints into a shallow dish with the lemon juice, olive oil, garlic, parsley and salt and pepper. Cover with cling film and chill for 8 hours, or overnight. Turn the meat in the marinade at least once.
3. Remove the lamb joints from the marinade and stand them upright in a roasting dish, pushing them together so that the bones interlock. Cover the bones with a piece of cooking foil, to protect them in the oven.
4. Press the split almonds into the meat at regular intervals. Spoon any marinade remaining in the dish over the meat.
5. Roast the meat in a preheated oven for about ¾-1 hour, until the meat is tender but still pinkish in the centre.
6. Meanwhile make the sauce. Put the egg yolks into a bowl and start to add the olive oil in a fine trickle, whisking all the time, as if you were making mayonnaise. Continue until all the oil has been incorporated. Beat in the lemon rind, garlic, ground almonds, sugar and salt and pepper to taste. Thin the sauce with a little hot water if necessary.
7. Serve the lamb on a roasting dish (foil · removed), garnished with watercress and accompanied by the sauce.

Lychee and ginger sorbet

Serves 6
**Preparation time: 45 minutes, plus
freezing time**
Cooking time: 3 minutes

1 x 425 g/15 oz can lychees in
  syrup

1 x 375 g/13 oz jar preserved
  stem ginger in syrup

75 g/3 oz granulated sugar

juice of 1 lemon

3 egg whites

1. Drain the syrups from the lychees and
stem ginger, and make up to 750 ml/
1 ¼ pints with water. Put the liquid into a
saucepan with the sugar and lemon juice
and bring to the boil stirring. Simmer for
3 minutes. Allow to cool.
2. Pour the cooled syrup into a polythene
freezer container, and freeze until 'slushy'.
3. Chop the lychees and 6 pieces of
preserved stem ginger.
4. Whisk the egg whites stiffly.
5. Turn the sorbet into a bowl and break up
the ice crystals with a wooden spoon. Fold
in the whisked egg whites, together with
the chopped lychees and ginger.
6. Pour the sorbet back into the container,
and re-freeze until firm.
7. Remove the sorbet from the freezer
30 minutes before it is needed. Spoon into
tall stemmed glasses and serve with
brandy-snaps or small ginger biscuits.

Chocolate and black cherry pots

Serves 6
**Preparation time: 45 minutes, plus
chilling time**

1 x 425 g/15 oz can pitted black
  cherries

100 g/4 oz plain chocolate

4 eggs

25 g/1 oz butter

3 tablespoons Kirsch or brandy

To decorate:

150 ml/¼ pint of double or
  whipping cream, whipped

curls of plain chocolate

1. Drain the canned cherries, use the juice
in a trifle or similar pudding. Divide the
cherries among 6 'petit pots' or small
individual deep glass dishes.
2. Break the chocolate into pieces into a
basin. Stand the basin over a saucepan of
hot water until the chocolate has melted.
3. Remove the basin from the heat and beat
in the egg yolks, melted butter and the
Kirsch.
4. Whisk the egg whites stiffly and fold
lightly but thoroughly into the chocolate
mixture. Spoon into the petits pots or small
dishes and chill until set: allow at least
4 hours.
5. Pipe a whirl of cream on top of each dish,
and top with chocolate curls.

Applescotch

Serves 6
Preparation time: 1 hour, plus freezing time
Cooking time: 20 minutes

450 g/1 lb apples, peeled, cored and chopped
50 g/2 oz butter
grated rind and juice of 1 lemon
3 eggs, separated
6 tablespoons whisky
300 ml/½ pint double or whipping cream
175 g/6 oz caster sugar
6 even-sized red skinned eating apples (quite large ones)
marzipan or chocolate leaves, to decorate

Leaf shapes can be cut from thinly rolled, green-tinted marzipan; or alternatively, lightly oiled bay leaves can be coated on one side with melted chocolate and then left to set — once the chocolate is hard, it will peel away neatly from the bay leaf.

1. Put the cooking apples into a saucepan with the butter and lemon rind. Cover and cook gently until the apple is tender, about 20 minutes.

2. Beat the cooked apple to a pulp and stir in the egg yolks. Cook very gently until the mixture thickens. Beat in the whisky and allow the mixture to cool.

3. Whip the cream until it is thick and fold into the apple purée, together with half the sugar.

4. Spoon the apple mixture into a polythene freezer container and half freeze. Once ice crystals have formed around the edge, tip it into a large mixing bowl.

5. Whisk the egg whites until stiff and then whisk in the remaining sugar. Fold lightly but evenly into the par-frozen apple mixture. Return to the freezer while you prepare the 'apple cases'.

6. To make the apple cases, cut a thin slice from the stalk end of each apple. Keep on one side. Carefully hollow out the centre apple flesh and core, leaving a 'shell' approximately 1 cm/½ inch thick. Brush all exposed surfaces of the apples with lemon juice, including the 'lids'.

7. Spoon the par-frozen apple ice cream into the hollowed apples and top with the apple lids. Wrap each filled apple in freezer wrap or a small freezer bag, and return to the freezer until needed. Remember that the apples will need to be removed 30 minutes before serving, to soften slightly.

8. Decorate each apple with a marzipan or chocolate leaf.

Hazelnut roulade

Serves 6
Preparation time: 50 minutes, plus cooling time
Cooking time: 12-15 minutes
Oven: 180°C, 350°F, Gas Mark 4

5 eggs, separated

175 g/6 oz caster sugar

2 tablespoons golden syrup

75 g/3 oz ground hazelnuts

300 ml/½ pint double or whipping cream

1 tablespoon powdered instant coffee

2 tablespoons hot water

100 g/4 oz flaked hazelnuts

icing sugar, to decorate

1. Line a large Swiss roll tin, about 25 cm x 35 cm/10 inches x 14 inches with greased greaseproof paper.
2. Put the egg yolks and caster sugar into the bowl of an electric mixer, or into a mixing bowl, and whisk until the mixture is thick, light and creamy. If you do not have an electric mixer, you will find that the mixture will aerate much better if you stand the bowl over a pan of hot water while whisking.
3. Whisk the egg whites until stiff. Gradually trickle in the golden syrup, continuing to whisk. Fold lightly but thoroughly into the egg yolk and sugar mixture.
4. Pour the sponge mixture evenly into the tin. Bake in a preheated oven for 12-15 minutes, until firm but spongy to the touch.
5. Remove the cooked sponge from the oven and immediately cover with a layer of greaseproof paper, and then with a clean cloth that has been wrung out in warm water. Leave in a cool place for 8 hours, or overnight.
6. Whip the cream until it is quite thick. Dissolve the instant coffee in the hot water and whisk into the cream. Fold in 75 g/3 oz of the hazelnuts.
7. Dust a piece of greaseproof paper with icing sugar and turn out the roulade, peeling off its lining paper.
8. Spread with the hazelnut cream and roll up as for a Swiss roll. Do not worry if the surface of the roulade cracks as this is part of its character.
9. Dust the finished roulade with sieved icing sugar and sprinkle with the remaining hazelnuts.

Cassata trifle

Serves 6-8
Preparation time: 35-40 minutes, plus chilling time

2 tablespoons custard powder

3 tablespoons caster sugar

600 ml/1 pint milk

6 tablespoons rum

15 g/½ oz powdered gelatine

75 g/3 oz mixed cut peel

3 thin sponge layers, about
   18 cm/7 inches in diameter

1 x 400 g/14 oz can peach slices,
   drained

To decorate:

300 ml/½ pint double or
   whipping cream, whipped

50 g/2 oz flaked almonds, toasted

angelica leaves

This pudding can either be made in a deep soufflé dish, so that it has straight sides like a gateau; or it can be made in a pudding basin, clean flowerpot or charlotte mould, so that it tapers from the base of the pudding to the top – in this case the sizes of the sponge circles are graduated, so that they fit the sloping sides of the basin or mould.

1. To make the rum flavoured custard, mix the custard powder and sugar in a basin with 6 tablespoons of the milk. Put the remaining milk into a saucepan and bring to the boil.

2. Stir the hot milk on to the blended cornflour and return the mixture to the saucepan. Bring the custard back to the boil, stirring until it has thickened.

3. Add 2 tablespoons of the rum to the custard.

4. Dissolve the gelatine in 2 tablespoons of hot water and beat into the warm custard. Leave on one side to cool, but not to set.

5. Lightly oil a 1 litre/1¾ pint pudding basin or charlotte mould. Pour a thin layer of the custard into the basin and arrange a few peach slices on top. Cut a circle of sponge from one of the layers to fit the bottom of the basin, and place on top of the peaches. Sprinkle a little rum over the sponge, and top with half the remaining peaches.

6. Spoon in half the remaining custard. Add another circle of sponge cut from one of the layers. Sprinkle over a little rum.

7. Top with the remaining peaches and custard, and finally the third layer of sponge. Sprinkle the remaining rum over the sponge. Cover the pudding with cling film and chill until set.

8. The pudding can be frozen, and actually served semi-frozen, so that it is like a sponge ice cream. To do this, remove it from the freezer 30 minutes before serving, and keep at room temperature.

9. Unmould the pudding carefully on to a plate. Pipe with whipped cream and decorate with toasted nuts and angelica leaves.

Coffee meringue gâteau

Serves 10-12
Preparation time: 1 hour 15 minutes
Cooking time: 50 minutes
Oven: 160°C, 325°F, Gas Mark 3

4 egg whites

225 g/8 oz caster sugar

1 tablespoon instant coffee

50 g/2 oz flaked almonds

Filling:

300 ml/½ pint double or
　whipping cream

25 g/1 oz caster sugar

a few drops of vanilla
　essence

225 g/8 oz raspberries

To decorate:

chocolate coffee beans

1. Mix the caster sugar and instant coffee together. Gradually add 2 tablespoons of the mixture to the egg whites as you beat them until they form stiff peaks. Add the remaining mixture and the almonds and fold them in thoroughly.

2. Line a baking sheet with baking parchment or greased and floured greaseproof paper. Pipe the meringue on the paper to form 2 rounds about 18 cm/ 7 ins in diameter. Bake in a preheated oven for 40 to 50 minutes until the meringues are golden and their bases are firm.

3. Remove from the paper and allow to cool on a rack. Whip the cream, sugar and vanilla essence together until the mixture is thick and smooth. Pipe one third of this over one of the meringue rounds. Cover with all but about 18 of the raspberries. Pipe a second third of the cream over them then top with the other meringue round.

4. Pipe the remaining cream in rosettes around the top as shown. Decorate these with the chocolate coffee beans. Pile half the reserved raspberries in the centre and stud the others around the side of the gâteau.

Chick pea and mint salad

Serves 8-10
Preparation time: 10 minutes, plus chilling time
Cooking time: 1½ hours

375 g/12 oz chick peas

salt

300 ml/½ pint olive oil

grated rind and juice of 1 lemon

2 tablespoons white wine
 vinegar

1 teaspoon caster sugar

3 tablespoons chopped fresh
 mint

2 cloves garlic, peeled and
 crushed

2 tablespoons sesame seeds

freshly ground black pepper

2 green peppers, seeded and
 finely chopped

3 large oranges, peeled and
 segmented

1. Put the chick peas into a large saucepan and add sufficient cold water to well cover the chick peas. Add a teaspoon of salt and bring to the boil. Simmer gently for 1½ hours.
2. Meanwhile make the dressing. Mix the olive oil with the lemon rind and juice, sugar, mint, garlic, sesame seeds and salt and pepper to taste.
3. Drain the cooked chick peas thoroughly and stir in the mint dressing while the chick peas are still warm.
4. Allow to become cold. Add a little extra olive oil to moisten if necessary.
5. Transfer the chick peas to a salad bowl and mix in the chopped green pepper and the orange segments.
6. Serve with a separate bowl of chilled plain unsweetened yogurt.

Smoked chicken and avocado salad

Serves 8-10
Preparation time: 30-35 minutes

1 x 1½ kg/3 lb smoked chicken
 or turkey

200 ml/⅓ pint olive oil

juice of 1 large orange

4 tablespoons chopped fresh
 parsley

2 cloves garlic, peeled and
 crushed

salt

freshly ground black pepper

3 ripe avocado pears

½ large cucumber, thinly sliced

sprigs of parsley, to garnish

1. Remove the flesh from the smoked chicken in small neat pieces (the carcass and bones can be used for soup).
2. Mix the olive oil with the orange juice, parsley, garlic and salt and pepper to taste.
3. Peel, halve and stone the avocados. Cut into thin slices and toss in the prepared dressing to prevent discoloration.
4. Arrange the pieces of smoked chicken, sliced avocado and sliced cucumber decoratively on a flat platter.
5. Spoon over enough of the dressing to moisten and garnish with sprigs of parsley. Serve with thin fingers of brown bread and butter or granary bread.

Baked cod and prawns en papillottes

Serves 6
Preparation time: 40 minutes
Cooking time: 1 hour
Oven: 190°C, 375°F, Gas Mark 5

6 cod cutlets
1 medium size head fennel
75 g/3 oz butter
salt
freshly ground black pepper
1 teaspoon dill seed
175 g/6 oz peeled prawns
12 unpeeled prawns, to garnish

1. Cut 6 squares of foil, approx. 23 cm x 23 cm/9 inches x 9 inches. Place a cutlet of fish in the centre of each square, and pull up the edges of the foil.

2. Remove the green feathery tops from the fennel, put them into a small bowl of cold water and reserve for garnish. Cut the head of fennel into quarters and shred finely.

3. Heat the butter in a saucepan and add the shredded fennel. Cook gently in a covered pan for 15-20 minutes until lightly browned and tender. Add salt and pepper to taste, and stir in the dill and peeled prawns.

4. Spoon the prawn and fennel mixture over the cutlets, including any butter juices.

5. Pull the edges of the foil loosely up and over the fish, pinching the foil together to seal, and forming a neat parcel.

6. Put the foil parcels on to a baking sheet. Cook in a preheated oven for 40 minutes.

7. Transfer the foil parcels to a serving platter and garnish each foil parcel with 2 whole prawns and a feathery piece of fennel.

8. Each guest opens his or her parcel at the table, savouring the full aroma of the fish in its fennel and prawn sauce.

Prawn omelette roll

Serves 8-10
Preparation time: 30 minutes, plus chilling time
Cooking time: 5 minutes

12 eggs
grated rind of 1 lemon
1 teaspoon dill seed
salt
freshly ground black pepper
50 g/2 oz butter

Filling:

300 ml/½ pint double or whipping cream, lightly whipped
300 ml/½ pint mayonnaise
375 g/12 oz peeled prawns
6 tomatoes, skinned, seeded and finely chopped
3 tablespoons chopped fresh parsley

To garnish:

few centre lettuce leaves
4 tablespoons mayonnaise
3 tomatoes, skinned, seeded and finely chopped
cayenne pepper

1. You can either make 1 large or 2 smaller omelette rolls, depending on the size of pan that you have.

2. Beat the eggs lightly with the lemon rind, dill seed and salt and pepper. Heat the butter in the omelette pan until bubbling, then pour in the egg mixture.

3. Cook over a moderate heat, agitating the mixture with a spatula or fork, until the underside of the omelette is set.

4. Carefully ease the cooked omelette on to a sheet of oiled greaseproof paper, and allow to cool slightly.

5. Place a further sheet of oiled greaseproof paper over the top of the omelette and roll up loosely. Leave until cold.

6. For the filling, mix the lightly whipped cream with the mayonnaise, peeled prawns, chopped tomato and parsley.

7. Unroll the omelette. Spread over the prawn filling, and roll the omelette up loosely.

8. Place the omelette roll on a dish, and arrange a few lettuce leaves around the edge.

9. Thin the mayonnaise with a little hot water to give a pouring consistency and spoon down the centre of the omelette roll. Garnish with the chopped tomato and a sprinkling of cayenne pepper.

Apple punch

Serves 8-10 glasses
Preparation time: 10 minutes, plus infusing time

8 lemon tea bags
bay leaf
8 cloves
1 x 7.5 cm/3 inch piece cinnamon stick
1 litre/1¾ pints boiling water
50 g/2 oz soft brown sugar
900 ml/1½ pints apple juice
600 ml/1 pint ginger ale
thin slices of lemon, to garnish

1. Put the lemon tea bags into a bowl or large jug with the bay leaf, cloves and cinnamon stick, and pour on the boiling water. Leave to infuse for 30 minutes. Remove the tea bags from the liquid.

2. Stir in the brown sugar and allow to cool.

3. Pour the cold tea into a large punch bowl and add the apple juice and ginger ale.

4. Add about 12 ice cubes just before serving, and garnish with slices of lemon.

Skewered fish hot dogs

Serves 8-10
Preparation time: 40 minutes, plus chilling time
Cooking time: 12-15 minutes

1½ kg/3 lb cod fillet, or other firm white fish

1 medium onion, peeled and cut into thin rings

2 cloves garlic, peeled and crushed

8 tablespoons oil

juice of 2 limes or 1 lemon

1 tablespoon French mustard

3 red peppers, cored, seeded and cut into 2.5 cm/1 inch pieces

Garlic butter:

225 g/8 oz butter

2 cloves garlic, crushed

3 tablespoons chopped fresh parsley

8-10 long crisp rolls or pieces of pita bread

1. Remove any skin and remaining bone from the fish. Cut the fish into 2.5 cm/1 inch cubes, and put into a shallow dish with the onion rings.
2. Mix the crushed garlic with the oil, lime juice, mustard, and salt and pepper to taste. Spoon over the fish. Cover with cling film and chill for 6 hours, turning the fish once or twice in the marinade.
3. To make the garlic butter, soften the butter and beat in the crushed garlic and chopped parsley. Add salt and pepper.
4. Thread the fish cubes on to 8-10 long skewers, alternating the fish with pieces of red pepper.
5. Brush the prepared kebabs with the marinade and cook either over a barbecue, or under a moderately hot grill. They will take about 12-15 minutes on the barbecue, and about 8 minutes under the grill. Turn the kebabs once during cooking.
6. Split the rolls or pita bread and spread inside with the garlic butter. Place a hot kebab down the centre of each one, removing the skewer, and garnish with onion rings, sliced tomato and watercress.

Parcel burgers

Serves 10
Preparation time: 25 minutes, plus chilling
Cooking time: 25-35 minutes
Oven: 200°C, 400°F, Gas Mark 6

450 g/1 lb minced bacon

900 g/2 lb minced pork or veal

4 tablespoons chopped fresh parsley

1 large onion, peeled and grated

2 teaspoons curry powder

2 cloves garlic, peeled and crushed

6 spring onions, finely chopped

2 eggs, beaten

salt

freshly ground black pepper

10 slices cheese, approximately 25 cm/¼ inch thick

10 spoons chutney

1. Mix the minced meats with the parsley, grated onion, curry powder, garlic, chopped spring onion, beaten eggs, salt and pepper. Chill for 30 minutes.
2. Mould the meat mixture into 10 neat burger shapes.
3. Brush the burgers with oil and 'seal' quickly on both sides, either on a barbecue or under a moderately hot grill.
4. Cut 10 squares of foil, each about 23 cm/ 9 inches square.
5. Place a burger in the centre of each foil square and top with a slice of cheese and a spoonful of chutney. Pinch the edges of the foil up and over the burgers and pleat together.
6. Place the burger parcels on the barbecue and cook for about 20 minutes (medium done), depending on how well cooked you like your burgers. Alternatively the parcel burgers can be cooked in a preheated oven for about 30 minutes.

Turkey and chestnut galantine

Serves 8-10
Preparation time: 45 minutes, plus chilling time
Cooking time: 2 hours 5 minutes

1 large onion, peeled and finely chopped

75 g/3 oz butter

100 g/4 oz walnuts, roughly chopped

1 x 425 g/15 oz can unsweetened chestnut purée

175 g/6 oz fresh breadcrumbs

salt

freshly ground black pepper

coarsely grated rind of 2 lemons

3 tablespoons coarsely chopped fresh parsley

3 eggs, beaten

3.5 kg/8 lb turkey, boned (see introduction)

To decorate:

600 ml/1 pint coating white sauce

30 g/1 oz powdered gelatine

600 ml/1 pint liquid aspic jelly, made from aspic powder or crystals (or 600 ml/1 pint clear chicken stock, thickened with 30 g/½ oz gelatine)

petal shapes cut from lemon and orange peel

sprigs of fresh tarragon

capers

Boning a turkey can be a fiddly job, so it's well worth asking your butcher to do it for you. He will be able to bone it neatly, without making an incision the full length of the bird.

1. Heat the butter in a frying pan, add the onion and fry gently until it softens and turns lightly golden.
2. Mix the onion with all the remaining ingredients to give a moist stuffing.
3. Fill the cavity in the turkey with the stuffing, and sew up each end with strong cotton or fine string to give a neat shape. For a really professional finish, tie the stuffed boned turkey in a 'sausage' of muslin.
4. Put the prepared turkey into a large saucepan and add sufficient water to cover.
5. Bring to the boil, cover and simmer for 2 hours. Allow the turkey to cool in its cooking liquid.
6. Put the gelatine and 4 tablespoons of the turkey cooking liquid into a small bowl and stand in a saucepan of boiling water. Stir until dissolved.
7. Stir the gelatine into the white sauce.
8. Stand the turkey on a cooling rack over a tray and remove any loose pieces of skin. Spoon the cooled white sauce over the cooked turkey to give a thin even coating. Leave on one side until set.
9. Dip the petal shapes, sprigs of tarragon and the capers into the liquid aspic and arrange decoratively on the turkey. Leave until the decoration has set.
10. Spoon a thin even coating of liquid aspic jelly over the turkey, and chill until set.
11. Serve cut into thick slices.

Potato and cheese tortilla

Serves 8-10
Preparation time: 25 minutes, plus
proving time
Cooking time: 35 minutes

1 kg/2 lb potatoes, peeled
salt
freshly ground black pepper
50 g/2 oz butter
2 egg yolks
100 g/4 oz plain flour
2 teaspoons made mustard
1 tablespoon Worcestershire sauce
175 g/6 oz grated strong cheese
2 teaspoons dried yeast
6 tablespoons tepid milk

Wedges of the tortilla can be kept warm wrapped in napkins or foil around the barbecue.

1. Cook the potatoes in boiling salted water until just tender. Drain well and mash with the butter, egg yolks and salt and pepper to taste.
2. Beat in the flour, mustard, Worcestershire sauce and grated cheese.
3. Sprinkle the yeast on to the tepid milk and leave in a warm place for 10 minutes. Beat the yeast liquid into the potato mixture. Cover and leave in a warm place for 30 minutes.
4. Brush a large frying pan or griddle with oil and put over a moderate heat. Press the potato dough out into a large circle, about the same size as the pan, and place in the pan.
5. Cook over a moderate heat for about 6 minutes until lightly golden and crusty on the underside.
6. Turn the potato tortilla over with a spatula and cook for a further 6 minutes on the other side.
7. Cut or break into wedges and serve hot.

Foaming hot chocolate

Serves 8-10
Preparation time: 5 minutes
Cooking time: 5 minutes

750 ml/1½ pints hot chocolate, made with milk but no sugar
600 ml/1 pint strong black coffee
75 g/3 oz soft brown sugar
300 ml/½ pint double or whipping cream
3 egg whites
175 g/6 oz caster sugar
powdered cinnamon

1. Put the hot chocolate into a large double saucepan with the coffee, brown sugar and double cream.
2. Stir over a gentle heat until the sugar has dissolved and the liquid is heated through.
3. Meanwhile whisk the egg whites until stiff, and then whisk in the caster sugar.
4. Pour the hot chocolate and coffee mixture into heatproof glasses or mugs and top each with a spoonful of whisked egg and sugar. Sprinkle with cinnamon and serve immediately.

Summer cheese pudding

Serves 8-10
Preparation time: 45 minutes, plus chilling time
Cooking time: 5 minutes

6 tablespoons redcurrant jelly

3 tablespoons brandy

12 slices white bread, from a large sliced loaf, crusts removed

750 g/1 ½ lb full fat soft cheese

100 g/4 oz caster sugar

300 ml/½ pint double or whipping cream, lightly whipped

20 g/¾ oz powdered gelatine

6 tablespoons orange juice

350 g/12 oz raspberries or blackberries, or a mixture

To glaze:

10 tablespoons redcurrant jelly

4 tablespoons orange juice

1. Put the redcurrant jelly and brandy into a saucepan and heat gently until melted. If the jelly is still slightly lumpy, put it through a sieve.
2. Cut the bread into neat fingers.
3. Dip two-thirds of the bread fingers into the redcurrant and brandy syrup and use to line the sides and base of a 1 ½ litre/2 ½ pint greased charlotte mould or soufflé dish.
4. Beat the cheese with the caster sugar and stir in the lightly whipped cream.
5. Put the gelatine into a small bowl with the orange juice. Stand in a saucepan of boiling water and stir until the gelatine has dissolved.
6. Stir the gelatine into the cheese mixture. When the mixture is on the point of setting, stir in the raspberries and/or blackberries.
7. Pour half the cheese and raspberry mixture into the prepared mould. Top with the remaining fingers of bread dipped into the redcurrant and brandy syrup. Finally top with the remaining cream cheese mixture. Chill until set.
8. For the glaze, put the redcurrant jelly and orange juice into a pan and stir over a gentle heat until dissolved. Allow to cool.
9. Unmould the set pudding on to a serving dish and spoon over the redcurrant glaze. It does not matter if the outside of the pudding looks 'patchy' as this is characteristic of summer puddings. The pudding can be decorated with whipped cream and extra berry fruits.

Iced strawberry fondant soufflé

Serves 8-10
Preparation time: 50 minutes, plus chilling time

750 g/1½ lb fresh strawberries, hulled

200 ml/⅓ pint fresh orange juice

4 tablespoons Grand Marnier or Cointreau

40 g/1½ oz powdered gelatine

300 ml/½ pint double or whipping cream, lightly whipped

6 egg whites

175 g/6 oz caster sugar

To decorate:

8-10 whole strawberries

8 tablespoons icing sugar, sifted

1 tablespoon warm water

few strawberry leaves or small bay leaves

1. Put the strawberries into the liquidizer with the orange juice and liqueur and blend to a smooth purée. If you have a small liquidizer you will probably need to do this in two batches. Alternatively, rub through a sieve.

2. Make the strawberry purée up to 1.2 litres/2 pints with water.

3. Put the gelatine into a small bowl with 4 tablespoons water. Stand in a saucepan of boiling water and stir until the gelatine has dissolved.

4. Stir the gelatine into the strawberry purée, together with the lightly whipped cream. Leave on one side until the mixture is on the point of setting.

5. Whisk the egg whites until stiff and then whisk in the caster sugar. Fold lightly but thoroughly into the strawberry mixture.

6. Either pour into a 1.5 litre/2½ pint soufflé dish, with a deep band of oiled greaseproof paper secured around the top, or into a glass bowl. Chill until set.

7. For the decoration, chill the whole strawberries for 30 minutes. Mix the icing sugar with the water and beat until smooth. Dip the tip of each strawberry into the icing and then place on a sheet of greased greaseproof paper and leave until set.

8. Decorate the top of the set soufflé with the fondant strawberries and small strawberry or bay leaves. (Remove the band of greaseproof if you have used a soufflé dish.)

Notes

1. All spoon measurements are level.
2. All eggs are sizes 3, 4, 5 (standard) unless otherwise stated.
3. Preparation times given are an average calculated during recipe testing.
4. Metric and imperial measurements have been calculated separately. Use one set of measurements only as they are not exact equivalents.
5. Cooking times may vary slightly depending on the individual oven. Dishes should be placed in the centre of the oven unless otherwise specified.
6. Always preheat the oven or grill to the specified temperature.
7. Spoon measures can be bought in both imperial and metric sizes to give accurate measurement of small quantities.

Acknowledgements

Photography: Bryce Attwell and Robert Golden
Photographic styling: Lesley Richardson and Antonia Gaunt
Preparation of food for photography: Anne Ager

This edition first published in 1986 by
Octopus Books Limited

Published in 1989 by
Treasure Press
Michelin House
81 Fulham Road
London SW3 6RB

ISBN 1 85051 388 0

Printed in Hong Kong